Sean and Daro Flake It 'Til They Make It

Laurie Motherwell

T0027208

methuen | drama

LONDON • NEW YORK • OXFORD • NEW DELHI • SYDNEY

METHUEN DRAMA
Bloomsbury Publishing Plc
50 Bedford Square, London, WC1B 3DP, UK
1385 Broadway, New York, NY 10018, USA
29 Earlsfort Terrace, Dublin 2, Ireland

BLOOMSBURY, METHUEN DRAMA and the Methuen
Drama logo are trademarks of Bloomsbury Publishing Plc

First published in Great Britain 2023

Cover design: Laura Whitehouse

Cover image: Laurence Winram

A catalogue record for this book is available from the British Library.

A catalog record for this book is available from the Library of Congress.

ISBN: PB: 978-1-3504-4072-2
ePDF: 978-1-3504-4073-9
eBook: 978-1-3504-4074-6

Series: Modern Plays

Typeset by Mark Heslington Ltd, Scarborough, North Yorkshire

To find out more about our authors and books visit
www.bloomsbury.com and sign up for our newsletters.

Sean and Daro Flake It 'Til They Make It

by Laurie Motherwell

Cast

Sean Connor	SEAN
Cameron Fulton	DARO

Creative Team

Laurie Motherwell	Writer
Robert Softley Gale	Director
Karen Tennent	Set & Costume Designer
Renny Robertson	Lighting Designer
Novasound	Sound Designer

Production Team

Kevin McCallum	Head of Production
Renny Robertson	Head of Lighting & Sound
Dave Bailey	Lighting & Sound Technician
Fi Elliott	Lighting & Sound Technician
Catherine Idle	Company Stage Manager
Scott Ringan	Assistant Stage Manager

Sean Connor is an actor based in Glasgow, Scotland. He graduated from New College Lanarkshire with a Bachelor of Arts Honours degree in Acting in 2017, and has since appeared in numerous film and television projects, including *Schemers* (Black Factory Films, 2020); *Still Game* (BBC1, 2019); *Traces* (Alibi, 2022). He is best known for playing series regular Dylan Christie in BBC Scotland's hit soap *River City*. His theatre credits include: *Moorcroft* (Tron Theatre); *Ode to Joy* (Stories Untold Productions @ Ed Fringe); *Until It's Gone* (A Play, A Pie, and a Pint/Traverse Theatre/Stellar Quines); and *Don Quixote: Man of Clackmannanshire* (Dundee Rep and Perth Theatre).

Cameron Fulton can be seen in Amazon Prime thriller *The Rig* as well as series regular Tyler Foulkes in BBC's *River City*. Theatre credits include: *Thick Skin*, *Elastic Heart* (Sonnet Youth); *The Benny Lynch Story* (Cathkin Park); *The Infernal Serpent*, *Do Not Push This Button*, *Confessional*, *Second Hand* (A Play, A Pie and A Pint, Òran Mór); *Blackout* (New Room Theatre); *Cinderella* (Imagine Theatre); *Cinderella*, *Mother McGoose*, *Aladdin* (Alhambra Theatre); *The Street* (Cumbernauld Theatre). Film credits include: *Limbo* (Caravan Cinema/Film4); *Our Ladies* (In A Big Country Films); *Connect* (Angel Face Productions); *Matriarch* (New Light Films); *The Eagle* (Universal); *NEDs* (Bluelight/Film4). TV credits include: *The Rig* (Amazon Studios); *Outlander* (STARZ); *River City* (BBC Scotland); *Scot Squad* (Comedy Unit).

Laurie Motherwell is a Glaswegian playwright whose work has been developed through the Traverse Young Writers programme and Traverse Breakfast Plays scheme, and his first major play *Sean and Daro Flake It 'Til They Make It* premiered at the Traverse Theatre in April 2023.

Also in 2023, Laurie was the Tron Theatre's Resident Writer developing a new play *The Grand Sun Shines Eternal.*

He has developed work with other organisations such as the National Theatre of Scotland, An Tobar and Mull Theatre, Macrobert Arts Centre, and Paisley Book Festival.

In 2019 Laurie was a recipient of a New Playwrights Award from the Playwrights' Studio, Scotland. Laurie is a graduate of the University of Edinburgh's MSc in Playwriting and a proud member of the Scottish Society of Playwrights.

Robert Softley Gale is the Artistic Director of Birds of Paradise as well as an award-winning and recognised writer, director and actor. Robert is an established figure in the Scottish arts scene, with over twenty years of experience. His award-winning writing debut and solo performance *If These Spasms Could Speak* was a hit of the 2013 Fringe and toured internationally to countries including Brazil and India. In 2018 he directed and wrote *My Left / Right Foot – The Musical* which won a Fringe First and Herald Angel at the 2018 Edinburgh Fringe and which toured to Japan. For BBC America he performed in *CripTales*, receiving two BAFTA nominations.

Karen Tennent lives in Edinburgh, Scotland, and is a graduate of Edinburgh College of Art. Her work as a theatre designer has toured all over the UK and abroad from village halls to Sydney Opera House. She enjoys collaborating with other artists exploring live performance in its many forms. Her design experience includes devising and designing physical theatre, theatre for young audiences, touring and in-house productions, as well as large-scale site-specific and promenade performances.

Recent designs include: *Thrown* (National Theatre of Scotland/ Edinburgh International Festival); *Castle Lennox* (Lung Ha/Lyceum Edinburgh); *Educating Rita* (Perth Theatre); *Man in the Submarine* (Perth Theatre/Byre); *Don Quixote* (Dundee Rep/Perth Theatre); *Muster Station* (Grid Iron/Edinburgh International Festival); *Field – something for the future now* an outdoor dance performance by Curious Seed (Edinburgh International Festival/Festival Cultura Inglesa Sao Paolo, Brazil); *Rubble* (Scottish Opera) a new opera by Johnny McKnight and Gareth Williams for Scottish Opera Young Company; *The Children* (Dundee Rep); *And If Not Now, When?* a film installation by Philip Pinsky and Karen Lamond in the National Museum Edinburgh for COP 26; *Christmas Dinner* (Lyceum Edinburgh); *First Snow* (NTS/Theatre PAP Montreal); *Lots and Not Lots* (Greg Sinclair).

Karen also co-directed *Sonata for a Man and a Boy* (Greg Sinclair), winner of CATS Best Children's Theatre. She also won CATS Best Design and was nominated for the New York Drama Desk Awards for Outstanding Design for *Hansel and Gretel* (Catherine Wheels).

Renny Robertson is the Head of Lighting & Sound at the Traverse Theatre. Lighting designs for the Traverse include: *Homers*, *Chic Nerds*, *The Trestle At Pope Lick Creek*, *Lazy Bed*, *Heritage*, *Right*

Now, *Arctic Oil*, and *Wilf*. Renny has also designed various productions for Lung Ha, Room 2 Manoeuvre, and Plan B. He has transferred work for the Traverse internationally including *Bondagers*, *Damascus*, *Outlying Islands*, *Midsummer*, and *The People Next Door*.

Novasound is the writing partnership of Audrey Tait and Lauren Gilmour. Since scoring their first short film for the BBC in 2016, they have collaborated with National Theatre of Scotland, Stellar Quines, Birds of Paradise, Royal Lyceum Theatre Edinburgh, Fuel Theatre and ItIsOn, amongst others. Novasound is Scotland's only female-run recording and production studio.

Their work has been supported by Creative Scotland, HMUK and the Audio Engineering Society. As well as being one half of Novasound, Audrey is the drummer in Franz Ferdinand and is currently touring worldwide.

Novasound are passionate about breaking down gender barriers in studio environments inspiring a new generation of exceptional female producers.

TRAVERSE THEATRE

Here we are – together – marking 60 years of the Traverse. Together, we celebrate six decades of stories that connect, inspire, challenge, entertain and that contribute to the cultural voice of our nation. With an abundance of shows from talented artists with urgent stories that bring life and vitality to our stages – both in-person and digital – the Traverse continues to be a platform for debate, a space for our community, and home of memorable experiences. Across our programme, you can encounter trailblazing creativity that offers unique opportunities to explore the world around us, connect with the lives of others and that spark that vital curiosity in what it is to be human.

The Traverse is a champion of performance, experience and discovery. Enabling people to access and engage with theatre is our fundamental mission, and we want our work to represent, speak to and be seen by the broadest cross section of society. We are specialists in revealing untold perspectives in innovative ways. This is our role as Scotland's premier new work theatre and a commitment that drives each strand of our work.

Our year-round programme bursts with new stories, live and digital performances that challenge, inform and entertain our audiences. We empower artists and audiences to make sense of the world today, providing a safe space to question, learn, empathise and – crucially – encounter different people and experiences. Conversation and the coming together of groups are central to a democratic society, and we champion equal expression and understanding for the future of a healthy national and international community.

The Traverse would not exist without our overarching passion for developing new stories and embracing the unexplored. We work with bold voices and raw talent – with an emphasis on the Scottish-based – to create the art, artists, and performances that can be seen on our platforms year-round. We invest in ideas and support individuals to push boundaries by placing them at the centre of their own practice, and through artist-led and co-created projects like Class Act and

Street Soccer: #SameTeam, we create spaces for stories to take form and grow.

We aim for the timely stories and creative programmes that start life with us to have a global impact, through tours, co-productions, digital life, and translations. We are critically acclaimed and recognised the world over for our originality and artistic risk, which we hope will create some of the most talked-about plays, productions, directors, writers, and actors for years to come.

The Traverse's commitment to bringing new and bold storytelling to global audiences is amplified in Edinburgh each August, when international audiences make the Traverse programme – often referred to as the 'beating heart of the Fringe' – their first port of call in a city overflowing with entertainment offerings.

Here's to the Traverse and all who have created with, played for, visited, and continue to champion everything we are. Our past successes drive our present and future direction, in the knowledge that our unique ability to nurture new talent and engage audiences through ambitious storytelling has never been more crucial in creating and sustaining a vibrant theatre landscape that reflects and challenges the world today.

Find out more about our work: traverse.co.uk

With Thanks

The Traverse extends grateful thanks to all of its supporters, including those who prefer to remain anonymous. Their valuable contributions ensure that the Traverse continues to champion stories and storytellers in all of its forms, help develop the next generation of creative talent and lead vital projects in our local community, Scotland and beyond.

With your help, we can write the next scene of our story.

Visit traverse.co.uk/support-us to find out more.

Individual Supporters

Diamond
Alan & Penny Barr
Katie Bradford
Kirsten Lamb
David Rodgers

Platinum
Judy & Steve
Angus McLeod
Iain Millar
Mike & Carol Ramsay

Gold
Roger & Angela Allen
Carola Bronte-Stewart
Iona Hamilton

Silver
Bridget M Stevens
Allan Wilson
Gaby Thomson
Chris & Susan Gifford
Lesley Preston
John Healy

Bronze
Barbara Cartwright
Alex Oliver & Duncan Stephen
Patricia Pugh
Beth Thomson
Julia & David Wilson
Stephanie & Neil
Drs Urzula & Michael Glienecke
Viv Phillips
Jon Best & Kate Duffield

Trusts, Foundations and Grants
Anderson Anderson & Brown Charitable Initiative
Arnold Clark Community Fund
Backstage Trust
Baillie Gifford Community Awards
British Council Scotland and Creative Scotland: UK in Japan 2019–20
Bruce Wake Charitable Trust
Cruden Foundation
D'Oyly Carte Charitable Trust

Traverse Theatre Production Supporters

Grant Funders
The Traverse Theatre is funded by Creative Scotland and The City of
Edinburgh Council. The Traverse has received additional support from
the Scottish Government's Performing Arts Venue Relief Fund and

Adapt and Thrive, part of the Scottish Government's Community and Third Sector Recovery Programme and delivered in partnership by Firstport, Corra Foundation, SCVO, Just Enterprise, Community Enterprise and Social Investment Scotland.

In Residence Partners

The Traverse has the support of the Peggy Ramsay Foundation/Film 4 Playwrights Awards Scheme.

The Traverse Theatre is further supported by IASH, the Institute of Advanced Research in the Humanities, the University of Edinburgh.

Challenge Project

Traverse Theatre is currently participating in Creative Informatics' Challenge project as one of the Challenge Holders.

Creative Creative Informatics supports individuals and organisations working across the creative industries in Edinburgh and South East Scotland to develop new products, services and businesses using data and data-driven technologies. The programme is delivered by the University of Edinburgh, in partnership with Edinburgh Napier University, CodeBase and Creative Edinburgh.

Creative Informatics is funded by the Creative Industries Clusters Programme managed by the Arts & Humanities Research Council with additional support from the Scottish Funding Council. It is also part of the City Region Deal Data-Driven Innovation initiative.

Traverse Theatre

Dave Bailey – Lighting & Sound Technician
Linda Crooks – CEO & Executive Producer
Marcin Dobrowolski – Customer Experience Manager
David Drummond – General Manager
Fi Elliott – Lighting & Sound Technician
Jennifer Galt – Creative Engagement Producing Assistant
Jenny Gilvear – Producing & Programme Coordinator
Ellen Gledhill – Director of External Affairs
Robbie Gordon – Creative Development Director
Becca King – Administration & Finance Assistant
Michelle Mangan – Publicist
Kevin McCallum – Head of Production
Anne McCluskey – Senior Creative Producer
Luke Morley – Production & Projects Coordinator
Gareth Nicholls – Artistic Director
Conor O'Donnelly – Marketing Manager
Julie Pigott – Director of Finance & Operations
Pauleen Rafferty – Payroll & HR Manager
Renny Robertson – Head of Lighting & Sound
Serden Salih – Digital Content Associate
Lauren Scott – Marketing & Media Assistant
Gordon Strachan – Ticketing & Data Manager

Also working for the Traverse

Debbie Bentley, Stacey Brown, Eve Buglass, Ruth Cawthorne, Rachel
Clinton, Lyra Cooper, Stephen Cox, Ian Cunningham, Leni Daly, Katie
Edmundson, Sandra Ferrer Garcia, Roe Fraser-High, Elise Frost, Avril
Gardiner, Noa Gelb, Laura Gentile, Jazmin Gilham, Bee Hayes, Darren
Hunsley, Jessica Innes, Amandine Jalon, Sam Johnston, Jonathan
Kennedy, Lana Kirk, Hannah Low, Mollie MacGregor, Jack MacLean,
Sophie Malcolm, Becks Marnie, Zoe Maunder, Matt McBrier, Alison
McFarlane, Olivia McIntosh, Michael McLean, Rachel Meek, Abbie
Meldrum, Danny Menzies, Tiger Mitchell, Afton Moran, Ellie Moran,
Nathaniel Morley, Chris Mundy, Aude Naudi-Bonnemaison, Dan
Nelson, Chloe Park Robertson, Zoe Robertson, Gabriele Schena, Eva
Shaw, Staci Shaw, Lev Slivnik, Rob Small, Heidi Steel, Colin
Sutherland, Eve Thomson, Odhran Thomson, Jessica Wain, Dominic
Walsh, Maritza Warnik, Katrine Widell, Rocky Williams, Alice Wilson.

Sean and Daro Flake It 'Til They Make It

for my family, my friends and Scottish theatre

Characters

Sean
Daro

(/) is an interruption. Dialogue can overlap at the Director's discretion.

(–) indicates that the following line should come in quick.

If you had access to an actual ice cream van and could perform this play outside, why not start early evening(ish) so it coincides with the setting sun?

This text went to press before the end of rehearsals and so may differ slightly from the play as performed.

An audience gathers around an ice cream van in a street, or a park, or the beach, or a theatre.

They can almost hear the jingles in their heads.

They can almost taste the ice cream on their tongue.

Sean *rolls a cigarette.*

Sean There's three things in ice cream.

Fat – that's the cream part.

Sugar.

And ice.

And maybe raspberry sauce. If you've been decent.

Maybe a Flake. If you've been good.

But what's *in* an ice cream?

The sun beamin down on your holidays.

A hinta blue sky, a break in the rain, the sleet, or snow.

No matter whit, someone somewhere, is having a cone.

It's in birthday parties. The pictures. Panto at Christmas.

It's in your freezer at home.

A couple of scoops shared on your first date.

Spread it on my nipples when we're gettin hot and heavy.

Then cry into it broken-up and broken-hearted.

It's in the van rolling down the tight streets of the estate.

Tunes played out tinny speakers.

Past the green and past school gates.

It's eating so much at Ikea you spew outside the spinny doors.

The last thing you get your dentures into.

That's if you last long enough.

It can be good and bad. Happy or sad.

For me, it's being led down Troon beach on an away day by Mum.

Battling gale force winds.

Sand stinging my eyes.

And right where it's meant to be, standing out against a grey sky.

An ice cream van.

An image burned into our collective consciousness.

My wee hands gripping the edge of the window.

Up on my tip toes to catch a glimpse into the secret world behind.

A hand passes me this sweet swirly pyramid.

Next thing, Mum's wiping raspberry sauce from my dirty chin.

The state of you, Sean.

You manky wee boy.

Daro *appears.*

Daro   Awright, ya dour faced fuck?!

You know whit would have been good here?

Some ice cream.

No just sandwiches and lukewarm sausage rolls.

Lighten things up a touch.

Know what ah mean?

Sean   I know what he means.

Daro   Has that effect on people.

That's what ah wis trying to tell you earlier, Hagrid –

Sean   The first random name of the day.

Daro   Mind? In the flat . . . Before the long cars came.

That ah wished ah'd had wan on me.

Sean   I was a bit preoccupied.

Daro   See, a cone is all ah needed to get that boy to chill.

When ah was in the green the other day.

I've no quite came all the way back down.

And no quite the other way either.

Sean   And this is what it's been like the last two long weeks.

Me and Daro.

His words washing over me.

Daro   The sound of kiddies playing. Dogs barking. Runners wheezing.

There's me sat, bobbing ma heid away to the sound of my own ears beatin.

This boy saunters over, breakin ma solitary silence, wae the gall to ask me for a smoke.

Daro *takes* **Sean**'s *cigarette.*

Daro   Bein the good Samaritan ah ahm. Ah oblige.

Then he holds it right back out at me. Out his mouth.

Wants me to light it for him n'aw like ahm ah walking-talking-zippo-man.

Sean   The audacity.

Daro   The sheer audacity, Sean.

Want me to smoke it for you too, pal?

No a peep. No even a giggle.

Just these blank eyes starin back at me . . .

That's when you know you're in trouble.

Sean   Sat in the flat amongst the rubble of a life.

Getting told tall tales I'm no longer part of by an old pal.

Daro   If you were there, you'd understand.

Sean   It's a you have to be there to know thing.

Daro   If you were there you'd have seen him with his nabbed tab plonk his arse next to my arse and start wafflin' on –

Sean   How awful –

Daro   How he's barred from most pubs. About bein in Barlinnie.

Aw sorts of shite.

N you know when someone isnae taking a liking to you?

No matter how many ciggies you offer them.

They decide. In that moment. There and then.

'Ahm goin to kick your cunt in . . . Pal.'

And he says, ah swear to God, he's some fucking nut –

Sean   If someone swears to God all the time, they ever tell the truth?

Daro   'You know ma name?!'

How'm ah meant to know this roaster's name?

Ahm barely holdin it thegither as it is, never mind somehow knowin this dobber's name.

He says, 'My name's Polo. Wanna know how?'

He says, ah swear to fucking God,

'That's the car ah wis conceived in.'

Sean   And Daro's chosen to tell me this long yarn whilst outside Mum's reception.

Daro   He's lookin into ma soul with them deid eyes.

Ma ain pupils vibratin back.

He asks 'You no gonna laugh?'

And I don't know if ahm meant teh.

Sean   Felt like I hadnae had a laugh in a long time.

Daro   Then these tanked up boys walk by wae blue bags bound for the bushes.

Polo points at me. 'Don't move a fuckin' limb.'

Sean   I wonder if his mouth caught up with his brain, would he just stop?

Daro   He's right up at these poor unsuspecting souls out for a quiet afternoon sesh.

'You know ma name?!'

Then they're howling hands on knees.

Mad Polo flies aff his mad handle. Cracks wan of them round the jaw.

So ah do what any good Samaritan would do.

Ah leg it.

And there it is, Francis. The van. Ma saviour.

Ah run up to it take a huge pole vaulter's leap, fly through the open windae.

Superman like.

Big Greg's looking down on me.

'Some riot called Polo's out there swingin fists.'

Ah ask to hide under the counter. Ahm no feart to admit it.

But it's no all bad.

'Cause ah get given a cone to calm ma nerves.

He holds an imaginary cone aloft.

Sean   Maybe when he stops talking he'd have said everything he's ever going to say.

Daro   You awright, Sean?

You listening?

Sean   Needed some air.

Daro (*smoking*)   Plenty of air out here.

Sean   Would be nice to have a little peace and quiet.

Daro   Cannae get much mair of that than at a funeral, can you?

Sean   Aye, you'd think . . .

Shaking people's hands.

Thanks for coming. Appreciate it.

A lot of noise.

Daro   People didnae half screech, don't they?

Sean   It's all chin up, son –

Daro   Bleak –

Sean   Take some time –

Daro   Tasteless –

Sean   Get away. Have some fun –

Daro   Wankers. The whole lot of them.

Sean   The world's your oyster.

Daro   Oh . . . Ah hate fish.

That's how I'd never work in a chippy.

Sean   What do I do now, Daro?

Daro   That's what ahm trying to say to you.

Greg telt me they're movin on –

In the literal sense. No the deid wan.

Sean   So that's what he's getting at –

Daro   End of an era.

He's worked that van since we were yay high.

Makin a livin on the open road.

Sean   Wouldn't really call their patch the open road.

Daro   Great wee earner.

Sean   Daro thinks he has business acumen.

Daro   Mind the time ah found that bottle of voddie and ah /
sold . . .

Sean   / sold it –

Daro   Aye, sold it tae / Tam Shaw . . .

Sean   / Tam / Shaw . . .

Daro   / Tam fuckin Shaw.

See, business acumen.

Sean   A fuck-up when he realised you topped it up with
water from the fridge –

Daro   Which wis your idea.

How wis ah meant to know it wis sparkling?

Sean   Ah said normal water. From a normal tap.

Daro   Ah wanted tae gie the boy quality water.

Yeh hauv tae learn from yir mistakes, Seany boi.

Sean   You'll have learnt loads then.

Daro   Ah've got a brain for business, me.

Sean   Nothing says business like a pair of trackies.

Daro   You can wear what you want when you're the boss.

You don't have to go to uni tae learn business.

Sean   I wasnae at uni for business.

Daro   It's no all essays, stories, books.

Or spreadsheets, stocks and dodgin tax.

All it needs is a little green to get going.

Sean   Just a little green.

Daro   That's aw it needs.

Sean   You're askin me for money?

Here?

The now?

Daro   You'll never hear numbers like it, Sean.

Sean   Fuck off.

You're no Branson. Or or Sugar.

Daro   Whit about Bannatyne?

Sean   Who?

Daro   That Dragon Den dick.

He started wae an ice cream van. Built his empire.

And he must've done well, Chandice, 'cause he's on the telly.

Sean   Wis on the telly.

Daro   And it all started wae ice cream.

You'd've thought it'd be Alan Sugar wae a name like that.

Sean   He shows me.

Daro   All this could be yours for ten grand.

A steal waeout actually committing a crime.

The van is as pretty as a picture.

In a run-down-nostalgia-trip kind of way.

Daro   Ah see you're sceptical.

Sean   I wonder how that is, Daro.

If it's the idea no giein me a hard on, or when you've chosen to tell me it?

Daro   Lovely big windae, or 'hatch' – technical term that.

Nice lovely . . . arches. Slushie machine. Mixer.

All top of the range, of course.

Big fuck off fridges, Sean – You need your fridges in this biz.

The van cost ninety-five grand brand new they said.

That's about the same as your flat.

Sean   Just 'cause it used to be worth a lot doesnae make it good.

Daro   The van's in good nick but.

And Greg's always liked us.

What with your recent hardships will even chuck in the remaining stock to gie us a head start.

Nice of him.

Sean   Awfy nice.

Daro   Mind the good times?

Summers buyin sweeties.

On the swings in the green watching it go by.

In your room and you'd hear the jingle and practically jump out the windae.

Sean   Driving Mum round the bend.

Daro   Then she'd gie us some smash.

Spend the rest of the day high as kites on pound mixes.

She was always that kind to me.

Some woman.

Sean   Bit different buying fifty pence mixes than a whole van.

Daro   Simpler times we can have again.

Sean   You're serious?

Daro   Genius is just amazin hings other folk don't understand.

Sean   Ohhh La Dee Dalai Lama –

Daro   Don't tell me the sky's the limit when there's footprints on the cuntin moon.

Pause.

Sean   Well ahm no interested.

Daro   Ah telt him we'd think about it.

Sean   You whit?

Daro   COME ON, MAN.

We need to take this chance by the creamy baws.

Sean   I cannae drive a van.

Daro   Ah'll drive.

Sean   You're gonna chauffeur me about?

Daro   Aye, Little Lord Farquhar. Cannae be cooped up all your days.

Think of the community.

Adoring crowds as far as the eye can see.

Sean   What vans you been seeing out and about recently?

Daro   Like something from back in the day.

An adventure.

Oh what a tale we could tell.

Sean   I don't want tales.

Daro   Sometimes a tale is all you need.

We're some team.

Sean   We've no been a 'team' for years.

Daro   And whose fault is that?

Always too busy to be home.

Partying by the looks of it.

Sean   And studying.

Daro   It'll be like riding a bike.

Sean   Except it's an old van.

Daro   What about Greg?

Sean   What about him?

Daro   Greg'll be able to retire. Pass on the torch.

He and his missus want to move to Aus.

Sean   Do they now?

Daro   You wouldnae be so cruel to take that away?

He heavy needs a break.

Says another ten years on it. As is.

During summer make four hunner pound a day minimum.

Minus four hunner a week we put back intae it.

Tidy profit of two grand a week.

Minimum.

The sky's the limit –

Sean   Thought there was footprints on the moon?

Daro   So?

Sean   You go for it then.

Daro   See . . . It takes money to make money.

Sean   I've no got any.

Daro   You've got the flat, but.

Sean   Mum's flat.

Daro   Ah mean. Technically . . .

Sean   And what would she say about using it to buy a van?!

Daro   What she doesnae know willnae kill her . . . again.

Listen . . .

Ah've been job hunting. Day after day.

Like our ancestors before us.

Apply, apply. Clickety click. N nae replies.

Let me read your meter. Deliver your mail.

Nothin. Ahn too many people looking at nothin.

Sean   You could work the doors.

Daro   Ah'd rather be inside gettin pingin' than standing at some door.

Sean   You could do the caring.

Daro   The whole world's dying on it's arse.

Ah mean . . . No offense, Sean.

But wiping rectums. Mopping up puddles of pish.

It's no fir me.

Sean   It wasnae for me either.

Daro   Ma granny was in a hame.

Mushy food causes mushy minds, man.

Sean   Actually think you'd be quite good at it.

Least my ears would get a rest.

Daro   Hearing aid beige. The whole place.

Life should have a bit eh colour –

Sean   You're no there for the décor.

Daro   Whit else can ah look at?

No Sky Sports. No a way to live.

Ah'll come wanderin' in. Everyone's face tripping them.

'Awright troops. Whit's happenin? Who the fuck died here then?'

Ahn they'll be like . . . 'Gladys . . . She's pan breed.'

That's some heavy stuff.

Sean   It would be something.

Daro   Is that all ah can do? Something?

Ask anyone 'Whit d'you do pay the leckie?'

When do they ever say 'Och, just sumthin?'

That's what shitebags with shite jobs say.

Do a job you enjoy, they say, never work a day in your life.

Sean   Biggest lie we're ever told.

Daro   You had a route set out for you.

Go to uni. Get a degree. Get a job in an office. Or whatever.

Haven't ah been wae you in your time of need?

Done ma duty as your best pal?

Sean   Awright.

Daro   When I was wee you and your mum were always there for me, Sean.

Nowhere else to be.

So I'm paying both of you back.

She'd love it. The two of us together again.

Sean   How would ah get a loan for a van?

Daro   Aye. Times're hard, int they?

And ah know just the place to go when times're hard.

Sean   Therapy?

Daro   Naw. The bank.

Like, now.

Sean   Now?

Daro   No time like the present.

And time is money.

Sean   The guests . . . the food, the flowers, the – the –

Daro   The – the – the whit?

They'll soak it up.

Sean   The bank he says.

In my Slater's suit.

I'll tell you now. This is no a real bank.

Daro (*as* **Findlay**)   Welcome to Findlay's Financial Solutions.

'Where your credit. Is our interest.'

Sean   For Fuck Sake –

Findlay   Ahm Findlay.

Sean   Are yeh now?

Findlay   Owner of this totally legit and fine establishment.

'Where dreams are paid.'

Sean   But you're no really.

Findlay   Near enough.

And can ah just say, from me, to you, you're looking well sharp.

You may be one of my best dressed clients ever.

Ah like that.

Sean   Got dragged here from a funeral.

Findlay   Nae rest for the wicked eh, son?

How's it I may assist you?

Sean   My mate said this was the place to come.

Findlay   Oh. Pay day loan is it?

Holding the hounds at bay are we?

Sean   An ice cream van.

Findlay   In this climate?

Sean   Cheers anyway.

Findlay   Ho. You came here.

You must've thought there was something I could do.

Sean   I came for my pal.

Findlay   Go-getter is he?

Great thinker is he?

Sean   Bit of a prick actually –

Findlay   That's a bit much –

Sean   He seemed to think it was a way to make a living.

Findlay   What's his name . . . that boy Bannatyne did it –

Sean   So ah've heard –

Findlay   Before he got dead famous. On the telly.

This Daro character obviously has a real eye for this sort of thing.

Income?

Sean   No. Well, I was at uni.

Findlay   Studying?

Sean   Took some time off.

Findlay   Cannae take time off paying your dues.

Sean   Daro –

Findlay   Good lad –

Sean   Daro, seemed to think you could use my mum's for a loan.

Findlay   Your mum's?

Sean   Mine.

As of recently . . .

Findlay   Why didn't you say so?

What's your plans with said van?

Sean   Sell ice cream?

Findlay   Will yeh aye?

Sean   Mibbe juice?

Findlay   When I was a young man my mum would send me for single cigarettes.

Back then you could get anything aff the back of a van.

I'll give the money to two strapping lads such as yourselves.

It's bound to be a success.

All you have to do is pay back the value of the van.

Over time. Monthly.

Wae a tiny, tiny . . . tiny bit of interest.

And if it doesnae take off.

Don't worry. I'll be here tae mop up your melted mess.

Daro's *back to being* **Daro**.

Daro Dae it for me.

Ya big woos . . .

Sean *signs the dotted line. However that might look.*

Daro Oh my God, ah cannae believe you did that.

Sean But you . . .?!

Daro I'm grateful.

Surprised, that's all.

Sean What have ah done?

Daro Ah can taste the success.

Sean Didn't realise you can taste regret.

Daro *puts the name 'The Whippy Bros' on the side of the van.*

Daro Est 1999? Est?

What's estimated about it? You'd think they'd know what year they started.

Daro *crosses out the year on the side of the van and changes it to 2023.*

Daro Established. Estimated.

See what ah / did there.

Sean / This better no be a right fuck up, Daro.

Daro Cannae fuck things up when we've got our logistics.

Sean Dropping some pins on maps counts for logistics now?

Daro It's all we need.

Sean Except it isnae.

We got . . . mixture?

Daro A full stash.

The size of those bags.

Sean   Ginger? Sweeties?

Daro   Christ, aye.

We've got it all.

Sean   Petrol?

Daro   Diesel actually, Sean.

Sean   The cost of diesel.

Daro   Enough to *drive* you to tears.

A classic jingle plays.

You're allowed to play jingles out loud for twelve seconds.

Them's the rules.

Sean   That right?

Daro   As well as MOT and insurances.

S'like a big car, intit?

Except for the food certifications . . .

And the street vendor licence from the local council.

Sean   An awful lot to remember for selling some ice cream.

Daro   Ah well, just one of the things we'll need to get sorted, eh?

Sean   Suppose it is.

Daro   Twelve seconds is aw you need.

Isn't that right, Sean?

Twelve seconds. To play a jingle. To bring them in.

Twelve seconds to pull the perfect cone.

The easy bit is filling the barrel of the mixer at the start of the day.

Temperature gauge inside the hopper. Flick the switch.

Fill the thing with the freshest milk.

Gas cools the hopper down. Chilled milk drops into the barrel.

Churn churn churn.

Sean   The easy bit.

Daro   Learning some transferrable skills.

Pulling a cone should be tender.

Patient.

Like . . . pulling a pint.

Sean *starts to pull a cone.*

As he does, **Daro** *puts his hands on* **Sean***'s hips.*

Daro   Pulling a cone's like getting intimate.

No that you'd know anything about that, Sean.

Sean   Fuck off.

Daro   Use your hips.

Let the cream fall.

Silky and smooth.

Do a little dance.

Make a little love.

No that / you'd know anything

Sean   / Aye, we get it.

Daro   Least somewan does.

Sean   Daro.

Daro *peers at* **Sean***'s finished cone.*

Daro   No bad.

But how d'you get to Carnegie Hall?

Daro *chucks the cone away.*

Sean   No by chucking our product in the bin.

Daro   Another!

Sean   I'll learn on the move.

We're wasting time.

Daro   That's the spirit.

Now we work.

We contribute.

We distribute.

Sean   Right.

Do we, get in, the . . . front?

Daro   The fuck . . .

The front? The front?!

Sean   What would you call it?

Daro   The cab? The captain's chair? The cockpit?

Two pilots about to fly aff into the big blue beyond.

Two pioneers of confectionery consumerism.

The Wright Bros have nothing on us.

We have taken the wheel.

Put our foot on the gas.

Ice cream shall fall from dusk till dawn.

And you, our beauty will take us to exciting new places.

Far beyond the horizon.

Together, we will fly, Fiona.

And no look back.

Never look back.

For this is only the beginning.

A jingle cuts through the moment.

Sean   We crawl around the estate.

Streets ah've known a lifetime.

The green. There.

Greg's classic patch.

Past newsagents and bookies and pharmacies.

And we stop. And serve soft scoop.

Just like the van did when we were wee.

Daro   'What's that?' They cry.

'Ahm gaspin'! They shout.

Sean   As the sun beats down from Scottish skies.

Daro   'Gawd. It's pure boilin. Only a cone'll fix me.

Here. Is that wee Sean and handsome Daro?

Sorry about your mum . . .

Can ah ginger prick.'

Sean   Next we stop at Daro's granny's old home.

Daro   Gie it a gammy granny!

Sean   Which is ironic.

Daro   How?

Sean   'Cause you didnae want to work here.

Daro   S'different, Sean.

Somewan else has to deal with their sticky mess.

Sean   You're a fuckin animal.

Daro   An ice cream dispensin machine.

Here, this one just asked me for rum and raisin.

Sean   And?

Daro   It's a real paedo flavour, isn't it?

Sean   You calling our customers paedos?

Daro   Naw, what ahm saying is this one here, who has a taste for rum and raisin, may also have a taste for weans.

You ever thought, Sean, people who're suspected as being paedos should be given pedometers to like track their steps?

Sean   Can't say I've ever thought that.

Daro   Full of ideas, me.

Sean   The summer months *crawl* by.

Daro   Get your cream.

Get your cones.

Get your Bru.

We do it all. Floats, oysters and snowballs.

Fancy a double nugget, ya muppet?

Sean   There's this belief among consumers that 99s used to cost ninety-nine pence.

That could never be right.

Back when 99s were invented they weren't even using the same type of money.

So 99s could never cost ninety-nine pence.

Now you're more likely to pay three fifty.

Daro   If you're lucky.

Sean   So we charge one ninety-nine a cone.

Extra for hunners and thousands and other extras.

Daro   And until Greg's fat stash of supplies gies out we're making a tidy wee profit.

Sean   What we're doing is undercutting the market.

Daro   That's a technical term that.

All our prices end in point ninety-nine.

Ginge. Ninety-nine. Bar of chocolate. Ninety-nine.

Sean   Point ninety-nine is a marketing tool to persuade people they're spending less than they actually are.

Daro   And as Sean says, a lot of cunts aren't skadgy enough to want a penny's change.

Sorry . . .

No cunts . . .

Customers.

Sean   Ahm getting a taste for it.

There's this freedom and joy to the work.

No spitting out essays.

No listening to lectures.

Feeling I actually have a purpose.

From this?

From working an ice cream van?

That's no what was meant to happen.

What does that make me?

Daro   An entrepreneur? A businessman?

Whatever you want to be.

People come up wae fancy names for jobs to feed their egos.

Like communications operators.

Multiple occupancy transit vehicle pilot . . . (*Wanking sign.*)
You're a bus driver.

Sean   Who's calling bus drivers that?

Daro   Ah've heard people.

Sean   He's heard fuck all.

Daro   But that's no us, Sean.

We're the ones in control.

Sean   Money coming in.

Early mornings. Working hard.

Daro's boundless enthusiasm.

Daro   Tappety tap on the card machine and away we go.

Bringing ice cream vans into the twenty-first century.

Sean   For the reasonable price of 1.75 per cent per
transaction.

Daro   Whenever the winds blow or the sun shines, son.

Sean   Like a real business.

Daro   Cream always rises to the top, Sean.

Sean   Aye . . . But so does some shites.

This is our routine.

Past the shops.

Daro   Catch folk coming out the pharmacy wae dry mouths
from the drone.

Sean   I'm no so keen on that one.

Pop along to some care homes.

Park up at the parks during the day.

Could stay out by the green till sunset if it's nice.

Daro   Just like the good ole days eh?

Anything to get out the house.

We see you. Saliva seeping from mouths shaped fir it.

Laughin' and smilin'.

Guid patter and pop ups.

Might pitch up outside ma old hole at Maccy D's.

Roll up to that drive thru window. Blastin jingles.

I'm an ice cream van man now.

Ahn you'll always be a bunch of McFanny's.

Cannae wait to be out again the mora.

Tell me ah was right.

Tell me. Go on.

Tell me.

Sean   Fuck up.

Daro   Don't be scared.

Sean   You might've surprised everyone by coming up with a semi-decent idea.

Daro   I'll take that.

No just a patter merchant anymore.

Sean   May.

We make that tidy wee profit that Daro promised.

Findlay's paid.

June and July.

Daro   Same again.

Sean   August.

Daro   Paid.

Sean *pays* **Daro** *out of the till.*

Daro   You know, these months, if we were real lazy, could be a montage in a film.

Some upbeat sort of bop.

Nice sierra filter, so we look, tip top.

You know like a picture frozen here. Another there.

Me bein a bit of a tit. Your arms crossed watching on.

Me laughing at your frowny chops.

As we watch the two different types of people eat ice cream.

Sean   The lickers.

Daro   Wae their big flabby flat tongues.

Sean   And the biters.

Daro   Plunging their gnashers in like they don't have any nerve endings.

Daro *takes a can of juice.*

Sean   Ho. Take a note of that.

Daro   Barbara, I've always taken stuff from jobs I've worked.

Sean   Not when it's coming out of our pockets.

Daro   Take it out ma wages then.

(*Opens the can and drinks.*) Ahhh . . . feel it in ma fingers.

Sean   Feel it in your toes?

Daro   Cannae help but sit here and think of aw the dosh we'll be making.

Sean   Aye sure.

All that money.

Daro   How one day I'll be like look at me, in ma massive hoose, with ma missus . . .

Who's a, like, Brazilian model by the way –

Sean   Course.

Loads of Brazilians round here –

Daro   Well she is. So get it right up you.

There's me and her with ma massive boat –

Sean   You've never been on a boat in your life.

Daro   I want a boat –

Sean   Where're you going to put it?

Daro   In the water.

Sean   Don't be ludicrous.

Daro   That's a mighty big word.

Sean   Where?

Daro   Wan of the docks.

Sean   The deid docks.

Daro   Won't be so deid when ah hauv ma big boat there.

Ma regatta.

Sean   Nae bawhair Abramovich.

Daro   You're always so negative.

Dream a bit. You must have some dreams?

Cannae have a future waeout some dreams.

Sean   If, and if we can do this for a bit –

Daro   If –

Sean   If we make a wee bit of money.

Go back. Finish studying.

Move away for a real job.

Daro   Right. You enjoy your real job.

And ah'll have parties. Oan ma boat.

Everycunt'll come, and they'll be like

'Here Daro where's that guy you used to run the van with?

Shame he's not sharing the glory.'

Dunno, went back to uni to finish a degree he didnae actually like much.

Sean   Started so I should finish.

I don't want to disappoint –

Daro   So let's be **bold**.

That's how I get my boat.

Sean   Ice cream is the real money maker.

You can make three hundred per cent mark-up on a scoop of soft serve.

Daro   What about yoghurt?

Sean   Cannae stand the stuff.

Daro   Frozen yoghurt?

Even the sound of it.

Frozen. Yoghurt. Fro-Yo. Something in that.

We can make the ice cream organic or vegan or some other shite.

Sean   That's pricey.

Daro   It's quality people are looking for.

Like . . . organic milk.

Sean   Explain to me what organic milk is?

I mean how can one cow be more organic than another cow?

Daro   Chemicals –

Hunners of cows are jacked up on the roids.

Sean   Pish.

Daro   S'like eggs. Free range eggs.

Wild chickens.

Sean   They're no wild.

Daro   They're out and about.

Like us.

Sean   We can give them the normal stuff and charge extra.

Daro   That's cheeky.

Sean   Like what you did with Tam Shaw.

Daro   He was a big nasty wide-o –

Sean   It's business.

The cheaper the produce, the more money we're making.

Daro   Sean . . .

I don't want to cheat folk.

That's not what we're about.

Sean   No. Aye. Sure.

Course.

Just you know . . .

I can feel it.

This chill in the air. The last of the summer sun.

The cold nights.

The green's growing quiet.

Just these sad sack stragglers bracing themselves against what's coming.

All I keep thinking is I'm doing this for my pal.

In a clapped out van.

And what's on the line for it.

You know what I mean?

Daro?

Daro?

Daro (*to an audience member*)   Awright? What can I get you?

Sean   Always desperate to impress.

Daro   We've got the tastiest cream round these parts.

Sean   One of the big issues of doing business in the same spots.

Day in and day out.

Is that people get to know you.

Even if not by your name.

But by your face.

Because you have become recognisable as the boys in the van.

Daro   The Whippy Bros!

Sean   When you become recognisable that means two things.

You become part of the landscape and people care less you're there.

Or suddenly you're everyone's pal.

And no matter how much you undercut the market.

Your prices are just never quite cheap enough.

Unless you're real cold bastards that can be hard.

So no fucking freebies.

Sean *stops* **Daro** *giving out freebies.*

Daro   Thanks a lot, dickdome.

Sean   Whit?

Daro   What's even the point in having a van?

Sean   Thought it was to make a living?

Daro   But we can live a bit more than that.

They were prospective customers.

Sean   They werenae buying.

Can tell by the way they were looking at the van.

They're tourists. Scrounging.

We should be doing better than will they won't they looks.

We're not run of the mill.

Daro   You're right there, Sylvia.

Daro *flashes a new watch.*

Sean   What, the fuck, is that?

Daro   Like it?

Sean   How can you tell the time with the shine off that thing?

Daro   Ah like it.

Sean   You're buying that and there's a scratch on the side of the van.

Daro   It's these tight streets.

So many nutters on the roads.

People have an agenda against us.

We'll gie it some paint.

Doesnae look good drivin' round with a damaged van.

Sean   And who's going to pay for that?

Daro   That's what profits are for.

Sean   Or flashy watches.

We're short of – of . . . cans eh juice, Flakes.

Where was it we picked up that big massive bottle of raspberry last time?

Daro   Dunno.

Sean   If it's online it might take some time coming in and that.

We need it now.

Daro   Ah think, Sean, it's time to dive into the deep end.

For it to become really real.

Sean   This no feel real to you?

Daro   Ah've always wanted to break my cash and carry virginity.

Sean   Daro's always been ambitious.

Daro   It's an exclusive club so it is.

Toaty wee cards to get in.

Those guys dressed in black ready to bounce you back.

Fellas checking your receipts.

Sean   Some boy hands us a membership form.

Which Daro thrusts in my general direction.

Daro   The money man.

Sean *gets his photo taken as* **Daro** *gives him bunny ears.*

Sean   And there, on the back of my membership card, the two of us, together –

Daro   Fuck me, Hector –

Sean   Forever.

Daro   Some buzz.

Yeh ever been in a place like it?

Sean   You know in a sweetie shop –

Daro   Or the side of a van –

Sean   And your eyes keep travelling up and up.

Following the rows of boxes. Treats and treats piled high –

Here. No running off.

Daro   The trolley's are dyin to be ridden.

Sean   This is work.

No a wander.

Daro   Ahm always by your side.

Sean   He says scooting aff into the darkness.

Now, you don't get mixture here.

You buy that from a specialist retailer.

But cans, crisps, sweets.

This is the place –

Daro *reappears.*

Daro   They're no real Flakes Sean.

Sean   Fuck me.

Daro   They're fake Flakes.

Sean   So?

Daro   They didnae crumble like real Flakes.

Know what ah mean?

Cunts'll know the difference –

Sean   Customers –

Daro   Your maw ever buy you an advent calendar?

Sean   Aye.

Daro   The chocolate's no the same.

And leave fruit and nut. Nae prick likes fruit and nut.

Here, there's some tasters over there.

You ever tried lychee?

Sean   Don't you dare.

I put it all on plastic.

A receipt as long as my arm spat out the machine.

And a price that blows the air from our cheeks.

OooOOhhhhffftttttt.

Daro *moves the stock.*

Daro   Hefty stuff.

Ah don't think you realise how much room boxes take up.

Sean   Pricey.

These numbers. They don't work.

Daro   I've always struggled wae numbers myself.

Sean   The prices we have.

They're too low.

Daro   That's how we're getting business.

Sean   We stay like this we'll be out of business.

Daro   You're only saying that cause of that receipt.

You're worrying too much.

Sean   That's the job.

Daro   Ah know what the job is.

Ah found us the job.

Daro *turns the key.*

Come on baby.

Purr for daddy.

The van stutters into life.

Sean   When autumn comes, sunny days at the green and on the streets, have been replaced with dull desk days.

'Cause school is back in swing.

Daro   A new hunting ground.

Sean   You cannae say things like that.

Not here.

A lunch bell rings.

Daro   A can ay Bru, pastilles, and a bag of salt and vinegar McCoys.

Sweets and treats flying aff the shelf.

Sean   Push. The. Cream.

Daro   Weans don't buy ice cream at school.

Some prick would slam it into your face.

Blowing cream bubbles out your snozz till hame time.

Instead we could be serving three courses.

Chips and hot dogs.

Breakfast down to dinner.

Sean   At twelve o'clock in the afternoon we find ourselves outside school gates.

Daro   The old stomping ground eh, Sean?

Same uniforms. Same vibes. Same grey clad walls.

Inspiring stuff.

Sean   Years after managing to leave this place and I'm back.

Daro   Triumphant though.

You're a business man now.

Sean   Taking cash aff weans who cannae be arsed walking to the shops.

Arguing with them about the price of a can of juice.

Daro   Doesnae matter if your big sister was in ma year, ya wee toerag.

Cash on the counter first.

Sean   Arguing how much a Freddo is.

Daro   Don't say that.

Sean   What?

Daro   Like how much Freddos are.

Sean   That's what everyone says.

Daro   Only dicks wae no other reference points.

Like the size of Curly Wurlys, or the number ay triangles in a Toblerone.

Sean   Well it's right.

That's how you see where we are as a society.

By the cost of sweeties.

Daro   But we're better than that.

We're in the know.

Sean   And whilst we debate the intricacies of chocolate based consumer economics.

Striding through the school gates –

Both   Is the Jannie.

Daro   He always was a proper sour puss, wasn't he?

Chasing you away anytime you wanted a tab by the bins.

Sean   A hard as fuck Jannie.

Daro   Genuinely looks as though he would crunch through bricks.

Sean   Genuinely.

Daro   The face of a man who has had to bounce back playground patter for thirty years.

That sort of pish will eat away at your soul.

Sean   Standing there with his arms crossed.

Big drooping mouth across his meaty chops.

Telling us.

Daro (*as* **Jannie**)   You two arenae allowed here.

Sean   How's that?

Jannie   Two hunner and fifty metres.

Off you pop.

Sean   Mon, you know us.

Jannie   So? Ah know all faces frae round here.

Still have to move.

It's the law.

Sean   Show us which law?

Jannie   Fuck knows which law.

I'm the fucking law.

Want me to phone the polis and get them to explain it?

Blah, blah, blah.

Sean   A right limp dick.

Daro   Suppose we shouldnae be too surprised ice cream isnae welcome round schools.

Healthy eating and such.

Sean   So that idea's gubbed.

Daro   It's crapmandu.

We still have the old folks homes, but.

They willnae be going anywhere quick.

Sean   They're no coming out at much pace either.

Daro   Diabetes is a fucking nightmare.

Nicking all our customers.

Sean's *counting out spare change.*

Sean   Living coin to coin. It's not enough.

Cannae pay the bills with pocket money.

Daro   Sure you can.

Sean   Not this small fry stuff.

We need heavy footfall.

Daro   Don't you worry, Sean.

Another fine mess I'll need to pull you out.

I've got an idea. But you arenae going to like it.

Sean   Why do you say something like that?

Daro   'Cause, Valerie, you have a tendency no to be a big fan of my ideas.

Sean   We're daen this, aren't we?

Daro   There's a Scotland game tomorrow.

Sean   No there isnae.

Daro   No here.

On the other side.

Sean   Who they playing?

Daro   Some other bunch of tight shorted wankers.

Don't know. Don't care.

But I'll tell you who does.

You know Murrayfield has a larger capacity than Parkhead?

Lots of bodies.

All wae deep pockets out that way.

They'll be chucking us full-on notes.

Sean   We cannae just rock up . . . Can we?

Daro   How no?

Sean   You'll have had to book it or some shite.

Daro   What's one van in the grand scheme of things?

Sean   And that's how we've found ourselves going down the M8.

The poor van nursed along on a Saturday morning.

Daro   Sipping at diesel.

Sean   A stale biscuit factory.

Metal statues cutting mad shapes.

Some fucking grass pyramids.

Daro   Heard that's a great place for picking mushies.

Sean   He would've heard that.

The traffic building as we get closer to the outskirts of our fair capital.

Daro   Stopping so much we should open up shop and serve ice cream to other pricks caught in the traffic.

Sean   That's actually a good idea.

Daro   I'll keep you right.

Sean   Some fucking weird looking building that's supposedly a casino.

Daro   And no a castle to be seen!

Sean   Instead these big fuck-off gates around the metal ribs of the stadium.

Daro   Big fuck-off-now gates.

Sean   So you cannae even get close.

Diving down side streets. Crawling through crowds.

Stopping every so often to pull a cone.

Sell a can.

Daro   Dig deeper, you cretins.

Sean   Shooting us looks as if they know we shouldn't be here.

Not part of the usual set up.

Outsiders disrupting some sacred space.

Daro   What's going on?

You lot not like ice cream?

Sean   The money is in the ice cream.

Daro   Whit bunch of weirdos doesnae like ice cream?

Think you're too good for it?

Stick our premium waffle cones up your tight as fuck arses.

Sean   There's nae money round here either.

Daro   You might be right, Mike.

Sean   The crowds disappear for the start of the game.

It's quiet.

Daro   It's deid.

They'll have to pass us on the way out.

No choice in the matter.

That's when we'll strike.

Sean   Least that's the plan until two new customers come to the hatch.

One who looks like he's pretending to be cheerful.

And another with the mother of all scowls across her face.

Daro   There's nothing worse than that.

Mothers . . . Like, on the computer . . .

Going tonto at some stupid hing they saw on the telly or 'cause their precious wean had their hair cut shite and she's telling her pals to boycott the place like – like fucking Israel –

Sean   Daro. Edgy edgy –

Daro   Evening, officers.

Sean   Melt me into the mixer.

Daro   Aye, that's us. The Whippy Bros.

This's our little adventure.

Best pals for years. Bloody inseparable so we were.

Sean *hides by pulling a cone.*

Daro   That mixer can be a right shitemare sometimes, eh Sean?

Ah'm the wan wae the magic touch.

Squeaky clean we are. Gotta be in this business.

You'd know all about that, eh? Must've heard stories?

Serious chimes.

The only branching out we're thinking of is yoghurt.

Sean   The back of my hair feeling guilty.

That feeling you get.

Don't even notice the frozen cream falling round my hands.

Daro   We'd be the worst criminals about.

It's such a quiet one today we might have to think about it.

That's a joke. By the way.

Funny how people can get so hot and bothered about ice cream.

Course we know you cannae be driving about without insurance.

And licences and the such.

Don't want to end up done.

My uncle's been in the jail, you know.

Says there's nothing to be scared of unless you've done wrang.

That's why he's always shiting himsel when he hears your sirens.

It's why ahm being open and honest with you now.

Sean   I think before I even knew what that feeling was.

I knew.

I'm wee again. On a roasting hot day in Tenerife.

My double scoop of vanilla has slipped off my cone.

And I'm staring down at it.

My face melting as the cream spreads over the hot ground.

Hoping Mum's going to replace it.

Which she did.

But now it's just us. Nobody to back us up.

And I've forgotten to get the street vendor licence.

Pause.

Daro   How about a cone? On the house? Wae a touch of raspberry? Or maybe not.

You wouldn't want it dripping over those high-vis jaikets of yours.

You'd look like a right pair of tits.

Sean?

It's our first time venturing out this way. Beautiful place.

It's been a hoot.

Go easy on us.

It was hard enough getting him out the house as it was.

Especially with . . .

Ah don't like telling people this. But his maw's just passed away . . .

Today.

And this was her van.

She loved it. Didn't she, Sean?

Serving ice cream and making the people happy.

And we must've. In the madness. Just forgot.

It was her dying wish. So it was.

That we come to serve ice cream to the good supporters of . . . the boys in blue at Murrayfield.

She was a big fan.

Let them have ice cream she said.

Her final words. Ah swear to God.

You wouldn't be so cruel . . .

Sean   They would.

Daro   Pair of boabys.

Sean   Two thousand pounds' fine for operating without a street licence.

Daro   How did you miss that?

Sean   Dunno.

Daro   'Cause to me that seems like a pretty big thing to miss out on when that's essentially the core of our work.

Sean   Ah don't know, Daro.

Daro   Like Al Capone with broken tail lights.

You think Banntayne would've forgotten ah thing like that?

Sean   Well, we're no fucking Bannatyne.

We're just wee fucking boys playing at running a van.

Daro   You ragin?

Sean   Then there you are making up all that shite about Mum.

Daro   Ah was trying to get us out a sticky situation.

She'd have found all this dead funny –

Fuck ah mean . . . You know what ah mean.

Sean   She'd have thought we were thick as mince.

Forgetting something so simple.

Daro   Well, I telt you we needed it.

Sean   Why didn't you do anything about it?

Daro   You know that's no my forte.

Sean   It's never been.

Daro   What do you mean by that?

Sean   Nuthin.

Daro   We'll figure it out.

Take it out what we have.

Sean   We've barely got enough to pay the fine.

Daro   We'll make it back.

Re-stock. And make it back.

Eh, Sean?

They pull into Harthill Services. **Daro** *fills the fuel tank.*

The rain and thunder comes.

A jingle bleeds into the dark.

Sean   Of all the places to feel like I'm having a heart attack.

It had to be here.

Daro   And they say that we charge too much.

The prices in there.

Sean   It had to be Harthill Services.

Daro   Sharthill mair like.

Sean   Where dreams come to die.

Daro   This engine's thirsty.

Sean   You want a detailed version of our accounts, Daro?

Daro   Not particularly.

Sean   I'll say it simply.

With our next payment due.

That fine.

The petrol –

Daro   Diesel –

Sean   We're on our last legs.

Daro   Keep it chill, Cyril.

I didn't know things were that bad.

Sean   It's grim.

Daro   It'll brighten up.

Sean   When?

Daro   Eventually.

Sean   This is the shite we have to deal with until then?

Daro   It wouldnae be right having a van without a drop of rain.

Comes with the territory.

Sean   Supposed to be safe and sound back on home ground.

But less secure than ever.

Wrecked and skint.

All reserves gone.

Daro   Have a can.

He doesn't.

Daro   Cannae even be innocent selling ice cream these days?

What's the world coming tae?

Ah suppose that's all part of it but.

Like when shite things happen and when you look back that's actually what makes the experience memorable.

No what you wanted to do originally. But the fuck-ups along the way.

And you remember and have a right old laugh.

Once it's all OK.

Sean   When will it be OK?

Daro   Dunno.

Sean   So we just go on.

The same?

Daro   Ticking over.

Sean   To experience the total shite bits.

And then, maybe just maybe, have a laugh.

Daro   Maybe that's how it'll always be.

The graft. The hard work and that.

You know?

Greg selling his ice cream in the green.

The mixes. The cans.

Strawberry laces. That we'd tie up and hit each other with.

Daen stupid stuff wae sherbet. Mind?

Bet he had hard times too.

And he kept going. Now he gets to go to Aus.

Sean   With ma money.

Daro   Done well hasn't he?

Sean   We can do better.

We need to stand out.

Daro   We do.

Sean   But more.

What was it you said?

Daro Ah do say a lot.

Sean We want people to take notice of us.

So . . . we turn it into a story.

A tale.

Sean *pulls out a small baggie.*

Daro The fuck you got there?

Sean Only following your lead.

Daro Don't think now's the time.

Sean No. We're 'selling' it.

Daro We could get into serious trouble with that.

Sean It's no real.

Sean *sticks his finger in the bag and sucks it.*

Sean It's sherbet.

Sherbet.

It's a different crowd.

A different time.

And we could use different colours.

Blue. Pink.

Popping candy for the adventurous.

Daro Cannae be legal.

Sean How?

Daro 'Cause.

We barely got away from the polis as it was.

Sean It's our story.

Our bit of grit.

Daro   It's fuckin rocky.

Ah suppose we start selling single cigarettes?

Like all the auld yins go on about?

Sean   Well naw –

Maybe the chocolate ones?

Daro   They're banned.

Sean   Fine the little white ones? –

Daro   They're rank.

Sean   I thought you'd be keen?

Push out the boat.

You wanted a boat, didn't you?

Daro   Well, aye . . .

Sean   Be a bit edgy.

Go big or go home.

All that malarkey.

Be more like you.

Daro   I've created a fuckin monster.

Sean   Branching out from nostalgia into notoriety.

Daro   We're no some sort of gang.

Feels dirty.

Touching something we shouldnae be touching.

Sean   It's never bothered you before –

Daro   Even if it is just a joke.

Sean   No one will even think twice about it –

Daro   Aye, yer maw –

Sean   What about her?

Daro   You think this is what we should do?

Sean   We need to be set apart.

Like a USP.

Just to get people through the door –

The hatch.

Daro   You're sure?

Sean   Your man Bannatyne would be proud.

Have a dip.

How do I know you're sound if you won't taste the produce?

Daro *puts his finger into the powder.*

And sucks it.

Sean   This won't work without you, Daro.

And I don't know what to do. But I need you.

I cannae lose it.

It's all she could give me.

And I've risked it for this.

Daro   Fucking hell, Sean.

Way to dampen the mood.

Sean   Let's take the van out.

Daro   What out?

Sean   Out out.

Where folk go to have a good time.

Daro   To let loose?

To cut a rug?

Sean   To cool their rusty throats.

Daro   Punters desperate for banging tunes, frosty drinks and filled cones.

Aff their tits looking to wet their whistles.

Sean   Somewhere we'll make a mark.

Daro   A beacon for cream.

A raved up jingle plays through the vans speakers.

The boys are parked up on Sauchiehall Street, Glasgow.

Daro   Put down those pints.

Leave your voddie cranberries by the door.

Stamp out those half burnt tabs.

Get your lips round one of this before hitting the dancing.

The music cuts out.

Sean   And . . . nothing –

Daro   'Cept for some old jakey wae nicotine stains running through his beard.

Sean   Who shouts back at us from a doorway –

Daro   You sell macaroons?!

Sean   . . . Naw.

Daro   What's the fucking point then?!

Sean   This is what we have to work with is it?

Daro   Cool it, Tabitha.

The world marches to a different beat.

You wouldnae be seen dead out at this time.

We'd still be bevvying in the gaff.

Sean   The hours pass.

A fine mist spreads over this new world.

As the daylight fades, and fluorescent signs for bars and fried food cut through the dark.

A younger clientele stumble and shout from bar to bar.

We crawl up the one way street.

Pulling in at any queue where we can see the dehydration on people's lips.

And as each one passes Daro picks up.

Daro   Where you off to?

Sean   Feeding him more and more energy.

Daro   Clubs.

Sean   The real money is outside the clubs.

Daro   Queues outside The Garage.

Nico's. Mango. There's all sorts of Variety here.

Folk getting KB'd from Firewater –

Sean   Needing something sweet to soothe their broken egos.

Sauchiehall Street's started bouncing.

Some late night indie crowd.

Cheesy Quavers.

We loop back and start the route again.

The van comes alive with light and sound.

Daro   Poundin tunes frae tinny speakers.

Bottle of ginger here.

Bar of chocolate there.

You willnae get a winch after they Monster Munch.

Sean   And ah pull out the baggies of sherbet.

And ah chuck them out.

There's a cheer.

Daro   It's no what you think –

Sean   Don't ruin it –

Daro   It's just for a laugh.

Sean   It's gettin folk in.

And more importantly indulging in the high mark-up item of ice cream.

'Cause that's / where the money is.

Both   / Where the money is.

Sean   Well, it is!

Daro   Shooting their wads at us.

Sean   Figuratively.

Daro   A golden shower of coins.

Sean   All figurative.

Daro   Economics wan oh wan.

Sean   Business people you see on the telly have a lot to answer for.

Daro   It's heaving.

Sean   Ah told you.

Daro   The apprentice becomes the master.

Sean   And the place is alive.

We've got a crowd of our own.

Daro *clambers on top of the van.*

He pulls out two big glow sticks and holds them aloft.

Sean   Where did you pull those out from?

Daro   Ah've always got a stash.

A raved-up jingle version of 'Do-Re-Mi' plays from the van's speakers.

Daro
  Doe, a deer, a female deer.
  Get your double nuggets here.
  Now, a name we caw ourselves.
  Far, The Whippy Bros have come.
  So, a cone in your hand.
  Sauce to drizzle on the top.
  A Flake to dunk and scoop the rest.
  Just tap your card and away you goooooooo.

Again.

Everyone
  Doe, a deer, a female deer.
  Get your double nuggets here.
  Now, a name we call ourselves.
  Far, The Whippy Bros have come.
  So, a cone in your hand.
  Sauce to drizzle on the top.
  A Flake to dunk and scoop the rest.
  Just tap your card and away you gooooooooo.

Daro *falls off the van.*

He reappears with his arms raised yelling with guttural triumph.

Sean   Daro?

Daro?!

Daro   Ahm fine.

Sean   What's the time?!

Daro   Don't know, mate.

Cannae tell the time on this thing.

Sean   Before we know it . . .

Four in the morning.

Legs proper rock solid.

Head buzzing.

Churned up, spat out.

Finish packing up and give myself a well-earned ciggie break.

Daro   This feeling man.

Sean   Burst.

Daro   Buzzin.

Tuned to the moon.

Sean   The moon covered in Daro's footsteps. Supposedly.

Daro (*to an audience member*)   What did you think of that?

Sean   Yeh, that felt / good

Daro   / No you.

What did you think of that?

Sean   Daro talks to some lassies we must've served earlier.

Having a right whale of a time.

Using his whole body to tell some tale.

Pointing at me as I'm packing up.

Daro   No bad for two young bucks like us.

All aff our own back too.

Mon.

Sean   Mon where?

Daro   Those lassies are inviting us to an afters.

Proper out. No working out.

Wind down.

Sean   Parks get busy on Sundays.

We gotta work.

Daro   We deserve it.

Sean   His leg's bouncing so hard his whole body is shaking.

Dancing to it's own tune.

Daro   We should be celebrating.

We can play catch up.

Sean   And leave the van where?

Daro   Where do you think? Here.

We'll find a spot and come back later in the morning.

Cushty.

Sean   Feeling total shite.

Daro   People work hungover aw the time.

Ah know a guy who took five Xanaxes and drooled into a fat fryer.

Us goin out for a couple of drinks isnae the end of the world.

Sean   I'm fuckin exhausted here and now.

Daro   You're no fun. That's what it is.

Ah wanna enjoy what we do.

Sean   Drive us back. Do what you want.

Daro   Whit and then trek back into town like a sap?

No thank you.

Sean   Ah cannae move the van without you.

Daro   That's what locks are for.

Take the money wae you.

We'll be back the mora.

Coming?

Sean   Naw.

Daro   Suit yourself shitebag.

Daro *goes.*

Sean   And that's how I'm here.

In some side street in town.

By myself.

At . . . fuck knows what time it even is now.

Which I have a feeling in any industry is probably the least safest place or time to be when locking up alone.

Sean *pulls across the hatch window.*

And he starts rolling a cigarette.

Sean   The early morning is dark and still.

And this guy appears. Maybe only a few years older than me.

And you know, don't you . . .

You get that gut feeling. That this isnae going to go well.

Like what Daro said, when someone doesn't like you no matter how many ciggies you offer them.

So I offer him one.

Kind of like I'm trying to say to this guy 'I'm no a cunt. I'm no a cunt.'

He asks about the palaver.

The singing and dancing.

The music. The lights.

To bring the business in and that. You know?

I tell him we're selling ice cream, cans sweeties, slush.

The usual stuff.

What it says there on the side.

One half of the Whippy Bros . . . aye . . . that's right . . .

Done for the night.

Closing up. My 'partner's' has gone out for the night.

That it's been a long hard day.

Taxi chat. I think that's what I'd define it as.

He asks, if we sell loads of stuff.

You have to sell all manner of shite these days.

Can't be a decent ice cream van and not have slushie, or sweets, or juice.

Least Daro has that right.

Ah ask if he runs a van.

Which was a fuckin mistake.

He did not take kindly to that at all.

'Do ah look like ah run a van?'

Mate, I'm burst. You could be a figment of my imagination for all I know.

And that's when he asks what's in the baggies?

Sherbet. Pal.

Just sherbet.

But he doesn't believe me.

It is.

Honest it was.

Here . . .

Holding out a bag . . .

And his fist collides with the side of my face.

Sean *is punched.*

It's like a sledgehammer smacking into my skull.

And as I'm falling I'm thinking . . . I've never been punched by an adult before.

And it fucking hurts.

And I can taste iron in my mouth.

Feel my eye starting to swell.

Ma tongue burst down one side where it's collided into my teeth.

I lie on the cold concrete.

Moisture pools from my eye.

Focusing on the glimmering shimmer of small crystalline shards in the tarmac.

Feel his hand in my pocket.

And I don't move.

Don't stop him.

It was only fuckin sherbet.

As he goes he kicks the side of the van.

And I just lie there for a second.

Wishing it wasnae like this.

Wishing that life could go back the way it was.

Before the van.

Before everything.

Sean *is slumped at the side of the van.*

Head ringing.

Side of face burning

Fucking freezing.

Shitting myself.

Cannae even think straight.

Too scared to phone the polis.

Ah just wanted something good. Something easy.

Fucking ashamed at myself for what I've become.

Fucking ashamed.

Low. Pretty fucking low.

When you're told you can be anything . . .

And you're nothing.

Where do you go from there?

And I must've dozed off or . . .

'Cause as this goes round and round.

The lid has come off.

There's light coming through the ceiling.

Fuck is that?

There's this thing against my back pushing me around.

I can't get out.

The current's too strong.

Then, I'm being pulled down through the floor.

Trying to hold on to the walls.

Trying to keep my head above the water.

But it's too thick.

It's too . . . heavy.

I can't breathe.

I'm sucked out the bottom.

Sitting in a premium waffle cone.

Held by none other than Daro.

As he's pulling more ice cream down on top of me.

Over me.

Swirling those fuckin hips of his as he does it.

It's coming up, down, around, creeping beyond my neck –

Daro!

Fuck me.

A giant Flake barely misses the top of my heid.

Raspberry sauce is poured straight down my throat.

He's raising me up to his manic face.

His tongue hanging out.

As he laughs.

The van rocks back and forth.

Sean *wakes.*

Sean   The fuck?!

A bare arse smacks and slides across the hatch window.

Titanic style.

Sean   You're a dirty prick.

Daro   Oh you know it.

Say my name.

Sean   Daro.

Daro   Say it again.

Sean   Daro?!

Daro *bursts out of the van.*

Pulling his top down and his trousers up.

Daro   Jesus, Sean.

What you doin there?

Sean   You're asking me?

Daro   Nearly gave me a bloody heart attack.

Sean   I scare the pants off you as well?

Daro   She – She didnae believe ah ran the van . . .

Let's no make a big deal about it.

Ah know, ah took the biscuit.

Sean   You've shagged the whole packet.

Daro   There's no need to be so crude.

Sean   What if you'd been caught?

Daro   Someone else watching us like you were ya wee creep?

Wae your beady wee eyes and your . . .

Here, what's that?

Sean   Leave it.

Daro   Someone's lamped you one.

Sean   What do you care?

Daro   Come on.

Sean   You left me to close up by myself.

Daro   Aye, but I didnae think . . .

Looks sore.

Sean   It is.

Daro   You should put something cold on it.

What you doing hanging about here?

Sean   I was sleeping.

Daro   That's dedication.

Sean   You think I wanted to wake up, here, like this?

Daro   I'm pure exhausted too.

Sean   No like you were getting any sleep.

Daro   I went to enjoy myself.

You won't even let me have a can of Bru.

Ah've worked in Fraser's canteen, Sean.

And even they give their staff a feed.

That's probably how you needed a kip.

Run down.

Sean   Ah was sleeping 'cause ah'd just got done in.

'Cause ma pal left me in town, at God knows what time, to lock up the van myself.

And ah got mugged by some random –

Daro   Tell me you put up a fight?

Sean   Naw.

Daro   Well, Sean, what do you expect?

It's a tough world.

Sean   He thought we were dealing.

Ah was terrified I was going to get chibbed.

Daro   Ah telt you didn't ah?

After all that 'Is this what my mum would want me to do?'

Then you want to perpetuate that pish?

She had higher aspirations for you than pretending to sell gear.

Ah know ah do.

Sean   Gie me your keys.

Daro   You think I'm going to drive away?

Sean   This is a big joke to you.

Daro   Have a bit of faith.

Sean   In what?

Daro   Me.

Sean   After this?

Daro   That wasnae ma fault.

You think me being there would've stopped that?

Sean   It would've helped.

Daro   I didnae get into this business to start battering folk.

You work in a chippy for that sort of thing –

Ah don't know why you're so mad at me.

You said ah could go.

Sean   But ah didnae mean it.

Daro   Did you no think pretending we were intae something rotten wouldn't get us into trouble?

It creates a fuckin vibe.

'Cause of course that's what we'd end up doing.

What everyone expects when they hear stories of boys like us trying to make a living.

And you've pushed us back into those stereotypes.

No me. You.

Sean   I had to make it work.

Daro   You never had to worry if it was the right thing.

No when it's so easy for you to step away.

Sean   I see.

A chance for you to bring me down to your level.

Daro   Not all people that swan off to university are smart as fuck.

Or have sunshine coming out their arse.

People like you are like cats. Always landing on your feet.

But your litter tray still smells ae pish.

Sean   You think going to uni is some big fuckin fix all.

'Cause that's what we're told. That suddenly it'll all be mapped out.

But it's no like that.

Once I'm done then what?

I'll end up doing the same job that I would've anyway.

Still trapped. Except with a degree.

I never got asked what I wanted to be.

No really.

Just told this is where you go.

Go.

I wish someone had told me to take a breath.

Stop for a second.

I wish Mum had.

Daro   Sean, you cannae wait for other people to tell you what to do.

You made a choice.

You chose to leave.

Sean   And I came back.

Daro   'Cause your mum was dying.

She didn't want to leave you.

But you left me.

You couldn't have been happier to get away from here.

When did you get in touch?

You were literally on the other side of the city.

Would've taken you no time at all.

That's proper shite from your best pal.

Sean   It's not my responsibility for you to make new pals.

Daro   Naw. But you should care enough.

Care like how ah cared for you.

'Cause I know what it's like to feel alone.

Where're your uni pals, eh?

I'm here.

Sean   And you're such a caring soul?

That's why you came to the funeral.

A shoulder to lean on.

You knew I was in such a state I would've done anything you said.

Daro   That's no true.

Sean   Saw your chance to slide your way in.

Knowing I was ripe for the picking.

Fucking snake in the grass.

Ah wish you'd have just left me be.

Daro   You were broken.

Sean   Thanks for coming round and fixing me, Daro.

Daro   Yir old da here came up with a solution.

Sean   Worrying day after day if we werenae going to make enough money.

Stressing out ma nut.

And all you've done is fanny around with my future.

Buy yourself a watch –

Daro   Which I paid for out of the work we've done together.

Me and you.

But you've only got yourself in mind.

Your maw would be spinning in her grave if she hadn't been cremated.

Pause.

Sean   She would. If she saw all this.

'Cause she wanted me to go.

Daro   Course she did –

Sean   Naw, Daro.

She wanted me to get away from you.

You were a bad influence. Going nowhere.

Daro   That's no true.

Sean   Why do you think I never saw you?

I knew you'd been looking for me.

And she told me not to.

Daro   But she liked me, Sean?

Didn't she?

Sean   What does it matter now?

She's gone.

Daro   Ah was glad when ah heard she'd died.

No for whit it was.

No like that.

But ah thought here wis ma chance.

And that's fucking rank.

'Cause I missed what we were.

And it'd bring us back together for a bit.

Until I knew you'd scuttle off again.

Eyes on some future ah wasnae part of.

When else was ah gonna get a chance to do something better?

Ah wanted something better.

Sean   Well ah hope this was it, 'cause I'm done, Daro.

I tried. I did try.

And look what happened.

Daro   What're you going to do?

Sack me?

You'll no get anywhere without me.

Sean *gets in the driver's seat.*

Daro   What're you doin?

Sean   I'm going to get down on my knees and beg Findlay
to get rid of your bloody van.

Daro   You cannae drive.

Sean   Cannae be that hard if you can do it.

Van related chaos.

Daro   You'll wreck it.

Gears crunch. The van jolts.

Sean *gives* **Daro** *the vicky.*

Daro *gets in the van.*

Daro   You've lost your fucking mind.

End up getting done for driving without a licence.

Again.

You maniac.

Sean   Don't . . . talk to me.

I don't wanna hear it.

Just drive.

Pause.

This should last as long as possible.

Really.

That long.

Daro   Ahm going to miss this.

Sean   Here we go –

Daro   No this.

No you.

Ah can tell you that right now.

'Cause we've had a serious fallin out.

But . . . there's something about driving perched at a higher level.

Makes you feel tall.

The bigger the car, the mair important you are –

Sean   Is the classic sort of shite Daro would spout as ahm trying to give him the absolute dogs bollocks of silences.

Brakes.

Sean   We stop at the lights.

And pulling out in front of us.

Full on frontal view.

A hearse going into the crematorium.

Daro   M. U. M.

Shaped out of pretty flowers.

Sean   Followed by a row of long black cars.

Daro   Long row of long cars.

Sean   Car after car goes by and in.

Daro   Popular person.

Sean   And the light's goin amber.

Daro's body shifts up over the steering wheel.

Hands tensed.

Knuckles gone white.

And he's revving the engine.

Then green.

And instead of straight on –

This eejit's turning right?!

Daro   Don't question it, Sean.

We're in now. No escape.

Prick move if we drove away.

Sean   Better than this at a funeral.

Daro   Said so yourself.

Ice cream would've lightened things up.

Sean   No, I didnae.

Daro   Sure you did, Sandra.

Sean   We follow on.

The most inappropriate thing ever crawl going into a crematorium.

Daro   Naw it isnae.

Sean   Tell me what's more inappropriate than this?

Daro   Well . . . .

Sean   We need to get out of here.

Daro   It's one way here on in.

We'd have to do a drive by.

Sean   Slink deep into my seat.

Fall into myself.

Heart pounding. Heat in my chest.

Rising up to my mouth.

Tapping the side of my head with my finger.

Like it helps.

Knees up to my chest.

Make myself small.

It's easier to hide and no be seen.

Looking at myself from outside myself.

Disconnected.

This won't last forever it won't last forever it won't last forever –

Sean *pulls his jacket over his head.*

Daro   The fuck're you doing?

Sean   You have to get me out of here, Daro.

I cannae handle this.

Daro   This is good for you.

Sean   I feel like I'm dying.

Daro   You're in the right place for it.

Sean   You're loving this, aren't you?

Daro   Ah mean –

Sean   You prick.

You cuntbag.

Daro *turns on a very loud jingle.*

Sean   Fuck fuck fuuuuuck –

The crowd starts to see us.

Turning round to stare as if in slow motion.

Daro   Anyone asks we're good pals wae . . . the deceased.

Sean   Good pals don't turn up like this.

Daro   They do if they work a van.

Sean   A sea of black and white.

All waiting to get inside to reminisce and mourn with respect.

A woman so upset, she actually stops crying.

Some kids hide behind them.

And scary looking men wae red eyes bulging, wae teeth clenched so hard the pointy bits of their jaws poke out.

Daro   Apoplectic they are.

Pure ragin.

Sean   He parks up.

Daro   In for a penny . . .

Sean   Daro opens the hatch.

The sanctity of this moment is completely fucked.

And it's all our fault.

A car crash image you cannae tear your eyes away from.

And Daro says . . .

Daro   We're heavy sorry for your loss.

Have a cone.

Sean   Daro grinning in a sort of –

Daro   We're here for you way /

Sean   / Or a –

Daro   Yir worries'll melt away –

Sean   Way . . .

Then . . . then this wee boy tugs his father's dark sleeve.

Brings him over by the hand.

They stand here at the hatch.

Red puffy faces.

The whole fucking lot of us.

Other than Daro here who grins his mad grin.

Daro   What you waiting for?

Sean   What?

Daro   Pull the boy a fuckin cone then.

Sean   So ah do.

Twelve seconds of excruciating silence.

And all I can think is . . . Stand stock still.

No sexy swaying of the hips.

How the fuck do you pull a cone with any sort of decorum at a time like this?

It's no the kind of thing you can do with real reverence.

Don't – Don't look them in the eyes.

As I'm holding out this cone.

This cracker of a black eye starting to show.

And the boy's holding his wee hand out towards me.

Ah squeeze raspberry onto it.

Stick a Flake into it.

And my eyes connect with his eyes.

And I've a vision of myself outside my own body.

In crystal clear 3D.

And it's no him standing in front of him.

It's me.

I'm giving me the cone.

And I wouldnae say it's happy. 'Cause it's no happy.

It's so deeply deeply sad.

But it's like some incredible thing.

Pause.

Daro   You could hang this moment in a museum, Sean.

It could be a poem a poet writes about way back when.

That sainthoods are given for.

Sean   . . . Saint fucking Sean . . .

Daro   Let angels sing for your sweet soul.

And may the creamy Gods be wae you.

Sean   Christ.

Daro   Hallelujah.

Sean   Lights flash as photos and videos are taken.

As this moment is remembered forever and broadcast around the world.

Daro   The Whippy Bros –

Sean   Handing cones out left, right and centre –

Daro   Would hand them up to heaven if we could.

Comfort and joy for the bereft and broken hearted.

Sean   And there's tears mixing with the melted cream.

Creating rivulets in the raspberry.

Their tears . . .

Mine . . .

Daro   It's an emotional moment alright.

No shame in that wee knob.

The mourners move on to wherever it is their moving on to.

In the literal sense.

No the deid wan.

Sean   And there's nothing left.

I stand there as empty as the machine.

Daro   Go on then. Ah know what you're thinking.

How much'll this stunt cost us?

We're no a charity.

And I'd say that kind of misses the entire point.

And you'll shout at me telling me that it's mair money down the drain.

That your mum was right. That I'm a waste of sperm.

But you know what? Ah don't care.

Fuck yeh.

Sean It was . . .

It's a lot.

You know, being back here again.

It's a lot.

Like . . .

Who the fuck takes pictures at a funeral?

Daro Cannae go anywhere these days without someone taking bloody photaes.

Poor memories, man.

Sean Who wants to remember funerals?

Daro Could be someone you're happy to see deid.

Then maybe it wouldnae be so sad.

Should've had ice cream at your maw's funeral.

'Cause, as someone who as there, it might've cheered things up a bit.

Sean Aye, Daro. Sorry it was a wee bit sad for you.

Daro It's good for you to come back here.

It really hurt you never came to me.

So you didn't struggle alone.

'Cause you didnae have to.

And I know why she thought those things.

Why she wanted to keep you away.

I think I always knew.

I just hoped I was wrong.

Sean I was busy too.

Daro But no that busy.

Sean   No that busy.

Daro   I want you to do well.

Even if that means no seeing you anymair.

So ah willnae stop you going back.

If that's what you want.

Won't even judge you for it.

Just so you know, it was never a skive.

It wis the hardest thing I've ever done.

Ah pure loved every minute.

Daro *hands* **Sean** *his watch.*

Daro   Don't really know what else to say.

Sean   I just wish you hadn't made such a big deal.

I wanted you to treat me as though nothing had happened.

Daro   But something did happen.

And it was nice getting to know you.

Again.

Seeing some of my best pal being himself.

So, you know, it's no all bad.

Sean *is back at* **Findlay**'*s Financial Solutions.*

Daro (*as* **Findlay**)   Look what the cat's dragged in.

Oh dear. The state of you.

Ach the terrors of the working world eh?

Here to pay me my money?

Physically? Like the good old days?

Big wads of cash.

Sean   I don't have it.

Findlay   Oh dear, oh dear . . .

Chewn up? Spat out?

I'm sure you gave it your best shot.

Sean   . . . We did.

Findlay   Sometimes you cannae win.

Yir wee pal. Aw, he'll be heart-broken.

But you have to look after yourself, eh?

Numero uno.

Dog eat dog out there.

So ah suppose you want a deal?

Scramble for your flat.

Hold on for as long as you can.

Eek it out.

For a start, I'll take the van. For a very reasonable price.

For me, that is.

There'll be a fee for the inconvenience.

Monthly.

And you'll struggle away and pay me back.

But at least you can move on, eh?

Sean   I'll sell you the flat.

Findlay   If you're no going to pay up I'll get it anyway.

Sean   Not if I sell it myself and settle up with you after.

If I do that.

You only get the value of the loan.

But this way . . .

You get a sweet deal.

I have some money in my pocket . . .

And a fresh start.

Sean *holds out his hand.*

Daro *takes it.*

Sean *pulls him in close. And puts the watch back on his wrist.*

Sean   Nae backsies.

Daro   You prick. You did whit?!

That's **bold** . . .

Thanks, Sean.

Sean   If you could go anywhere, where would you go?

Daro   As in our logistics?

Sean   As in our logistics.

But done right.

Daro   New pitches.

Islands. And ferries.

Music festivals.

Go international.

Take the Whippy Bros to Blackpool.

I've always fancied Cornwall. Or Jersey.

Heard the beaches are real swanky.

Or further afield. The sunshine state.

Sean   The Gold Coast.

Daro   Barcelona. Brazil. By way of Bonnyrigg.

Could sell gelato to the Italians.

Ice to the Inuits is old hat.

World's our oyster – cone.

Sean   A right pair of double nuggets.

Daro   Now you're getting it!

Sean   Fucking . . . Thelma and Louise it!

Daro   They no the wans that went aff a cliff?

Lights flash. Music blares. It's a right sight.

The engine revs.

'Here, we, fucking, go.'

Then, the engine fails.

They try again and it splutters back into life . . .

The End.

And now the audience should be given an ice cream cone.

Just seems like an awfy nice thing to do.

Printed in the USA
CPSIA information can be obtained
at www.ICGtesting.com
LVHW021439180224
772058LV00008B/242

9 781350 440722